Tasha Tudor

MOTHER
GOOSE

MOTHER GOOSE

Seventy-seven Verses with Pictures by
TASHA TUDOR

HENRY Z. WALCK, INC.

This Main Entry catalog card may be reproduced without permission.

CONTENTS

CONTENTS

To
Mary Denny
Burnett

MOTHER GOOSE

Ring-a-round-a roses,
A pocket full of posies;
Hush-hush-hush—
We'll all tumble down.

Here we go round the mulberry bush,
The mulberry bush, the mulberry bush,
Here we go round the mulberry bush,
All on a frosty morning.

Doctor Foster went to Glo'ster
In a shower of rain.
He stepped in a puddle,
Up to his middle,
And never went there again.

Hot Cross Buns!
Hot Cross Buns!
One a penny, two a penny,
Hot Cross Buns!
If you have no daughters,
Pray give them to your sons.

The north wind doth blow,
And we shall have snow,
And what will poor Robin do then?
      Poor thing!

He'll sit in a barn
To keep himself warm,
And hide his head under his wing,
      Poor thing!

March winds and April showers
Bring forth May flowers.

Jack and Jill went up the hill,
To fetch a pail of water;
Jack fell down and broke his crown,
And Jill came tumbling after.

See, saw, Margery Daw,
Jacky shall have a new master;
Jacky shall have but a penny a day,
Because he can't work any faster.

The fair maid who, the first of May,
Goes to the fields at break of day,
And washes her face in dew from the hawthorn tree
Will ever after handsome be.

My maid Mary, she minds the dairy,
While I go a-hoeing and mowing each morn;
Gaily run the reel and the little spinning wheel,
While I am singing and mowing my corn.

There was an old woman who lived under a hill,
And if she's not gone, she lives there still.

Rain, rain, go away,
Come again another day;
Little Johnny wants to play.

A swarm of bees in May
Is worth a load of hay;
A swarm of bees in June
Is worth a silver spoon;
A swarm of bees in July
Is not worth a fly.

Little boy blue, come blow your horn;
The sheep's in the meadow, the cow's in the corn.
Where's the little boy that looks after the sheep?
He's under the haystack, fast asleep.

Lady bird, lady bird, fly away home;
Thy house is on fire, thy children all gone
All but one, and her name is Anne,
And she crept under the pudding pan.

Here am I, little jumping Joan,
When nobody's with me I'm always alone.

Did you see my wife, did you see, did you see,
Did you see my wife looking for me?
She wears a straw bonnet, with white ribbons on it,
And dimity petticoats over her knee.

Oh dear, what can the matter be?
Oh dear, what can the matter be?
Oh dear, what can the matter be?
Johnny's so long at the fair.
He promised to bring me a basket of posies,
A garland of lilies, a garland of roses,
He promised to bring me a bunch of blue ribbons
To tie up my bonny brown hair.

There was a piper had a cow,
And he had nought to give her,
He pull'd out his pipes and play'd her a tune,
And bade the cow consider.

The cow considered very well,
And gave the piper a penny,
And bade him play the other tune,
"Corn rigs are bonny."

Humpty-Dumpty sat on a wall,
Humpty-Dumpty had a great fall;
All the king's horses and all the king's men,
Cannot put Humpty-Dumpty together again.

Three blind mice, see how they run!
They all ran after the farmer's wife,
Who cut off their tails with a carving knife;
Did ever you hear such a thing in your life
As three blind mice?

Mary, Mary, quite contrary,
How does your garden grow?
With silver bells and cockle shells,
And pretty maids all in a row.

Cackle, cackle, Madam Goose!
Have you any feathers loose?
Truly, have I, little fellow,
Half enough to fill a pillow;
And here are quills, take one or ten,
And make from each, pop-gun or pen.

Willy boy, Willy boy,
Where are you going?
I will go with you, if I may.
I am going to the meadows,
To see them a-mowing,
I am going to see them make the hay.

Hush-a-bye, baby, on the tree top,
When the wind blows, the cradle will rock;
When the bough breaks, the cradle will fall.
Down will come baby, cradle, and all.

Lavender's blue, diddle, diddle!
Lavender's green.
When I am king, diddle, diddle!
You shall be queen.

Call up your men, diddle, diddle!
Set them to work;
Some to the plough, diddle, diddle!
Some to the cart.

Some to make hay, diddle diddle!
Some to cut corn;
While you and I, diddle, diddle!
Keep ourselves warm.

Bryan O'Lin had no breeches to wear,
So he bought him a sheepskin and made him a pair.
With the skinny side out, and the woolly side in,
"Ah, ha! that is warm!" said Bryan O'Lin.

Bonny lass, pretty lass, wilt thou be mine?
Thou shalt not wash dishes,
Nor yet feed the swine;
Thou shalt sit on a cushion, and sew a fine seam,
And thou shalt eat strawberries, sugar and cream!

When good King Arthur ruled this land,
He was a goodly king.
He stole three pecks of barley meal,
To make a bag pudding.

A bag pudding the Queen did make,
And stuffed it well with plums,
And in it put great lumps of fat,
As big as my two thumbs.

The King and Queen did eat thereof,
And noblemen beside,
And what they could not eat that night,
The Queen next morning fried.

There was an old woman who lived in a shoe,
She had so many children she didn't know what to do;
She gave them some broth without any bread;
She whipped them all soundly and put them to bed.

Jack be nimble, Jack be quick,
Jack jump over the candle stick.

Deedle, deedle, dumpling, my son John,
Went to bed with his breeches on;
One shoe off, and one shoe on,
Deedle, deedle, dumpling, my son John.

Little Bo-Peep, she lost her sheep,
And didn't know where to find them;
Let them alone, they'll all come home,
And bring their tails behind them.

Baa, baa, black sheep,
Have you any wool?
Yes, marry, have I,
Three bags full:
One for my master,
And one for my dame,
But none for the little boy
Who cries in the lane.

Cock a doodle doo!
My dame has lost her shoe;
My master's lost his fiddling stick,
And don't know what to do.

Simple Simon met a pieman
Going to the fair.
Says Simple Simon to the pieman,
"Let me taste your ware."

Says the pieman to Simple Simon,
"Show me first your penny."
Says Simple Simon to the pieman,
"Indeed, I have not any."

"Where are you going to, my pretty maid?"
"I'm going a-milking, sir," she said.

"May I go with you, my pretty maid?"
"Yes, if you please, kind sir," she said.

"What is your father, my pretty maid?"
"My father's a farmer, sir," she said.

"What is your fortune, my pretty maid?"
"My face is my fortune, sir," she said.

"Then I can't marry you, my pretty maid."
"Nobody asked you, sir!" she said.

Margaret wrote a letter,
Sealed it with her finger,
Threw it in the dam
For the dusty miller.

Dusty was his coat,
Dusty was his siller,
Dusty was the kiss
I'd from the dusty miller.

If I had my pockets
Full of gold and siller,
I would give it all
To my dusty miller.

Little Tom Tucker
Sings for his supper;
What shall he eat?
White bread and butter.
How shall he cut it
Without e'er a knife?
How will he be married
Without e'er a wife?

Hickety, pickety, my black hen,
She lays fine eggs for gentlemen;
Gentlemen come every day,
To see what my black hen doth lay.

The Queen of Hearts
She made some tarts,
All on a summer's day.
The Knave of Hearts,
He stole those tarts,
And took them clean away.

The King of Hearts
Called for the tarts,
And beat the Knave full sore;
The Knave of Hearts
Brought back those tarts,
And vow'd he'd steal no more.

Old King Cole was a merry old soul,
And a merry old soul was he;
He called for his pipe,
And he called for his bowl,
And he called for his fiddlers three.

Every fiddler, he had a fiddle,
And a very fine fiddle had he;
Twee tweedle dee, tweedle dee, went the fiddles.
Oh, there's none so rare,
As can compare
With King Cole and his fiddlers three!

Georgey Porgey, pudding and pie,
Kissed the girls and made them cry;
When the girls come out to play,
Georgey Porgey runs away.

Pat-a-cake, pat-a-cake, baker's man!
Make me a cake as fast as you can;
Pat it, and prick it, and mark it with T,
Put in the oven for Tommy and me.

Little Jack Horner
Sat in a corner,
Eating a Christmas pie;
He put in his thumb,
And pulled out a plum,
And said, "What a good boy am I!"

Bye, baby, bunting,
Daddy's gone a-hunting,
Gone to fetch a rabbit skin
To wrap his baby bunting in.

Jack Spratt could eat no fat,
His wife could eat no lean,
And so, betwixt them both, you see,
They licked the platter clean.

Old Mother Hubbard
Went to the cupboard
To fetch her poor dog a bone.
But when she came there
The cupboard was bare,
And so the poor dog had none.

London bridge is broken down,
Dance over my Ladye Lea
London bridge is broken down;
With a gay ladye.

How shall we build it up again?
Dance over my Ladye Lea;
How shall we build it up again?
With a gay ladye.

Silver and gold will be stole away,
Dance over my Ladye Lea;
Silver and gold will be stole away,
With a gay ladye.

Wood and clay will wash away,
Dance over my Ladye Lea;
Wood and clay will wash away;
With a gay ladye.

Iron and steel will bend and bow,
Dance over my Ladye Lea;
Iron and steel will bend and bow,
With a gay ladye.

Build it up with stone so strong,
Dance over my Ladye Lea;
Huzza! 'Twill last for ages long,
With a gay ladye.

I saw a ship a sailing,
A sailing on the sea;
And, oh! it was all laden
With pretty things for thee!

There were comfits in the cabin,
And apples in the hold!
The sails were made of silk,
And the masts were made of gold.

The four and twenty sailors,
That stood between the decks,
Were four and twenty white mice,
With chains about their necks.

The captain was a duck,
With a packet on his back;
And when the ship began to move,
The captain said, "Quack! Quack!"

Who comes here?   Where is your money?
"A grenadier."   "I've forgot."
What do you want?   Get you gone,
"A pot of beer."   You can't have a drop.

I had a little nut tree, nothing would it bear
But a silver nutmeg and a golden pear;
The king of Spain's daughter came to visit me,
And all for the sake of my little nut tree.
I skipped over water, I danced over sea,
And all the birds in the air couldn't catch me.

Sing a song of sixpence, a pocket full of rye;
Four and twenty blackbirds baked in a pie;
When the pie was opened, the birds began to sing,
Was not that a dainty dish to set before the king?

The king was in the counting house, counting out his money;
The queen was in the parlor, eating bread and honey;
The maid was in the garden, hanging out the clothes;
When down came a blackbird and pecked off her nose.

How many miles is it to Babylon?
Three score miles and ten.
Can I get there by candlelight?
Yes, and back again!
If your heels are nimble and light,
You may get there by candlelight.

Pease porridge hot,
Pease porridge cold,
Pease porridge in the pot nine days old.
Some like it hot,
Some like it cold,
Some like it in the pot nine days old.

This little pig went to market,
This little pig stayed home.
This little pig had roast beef.
This little pig had none.
This little pig cried wee, wee, wee,
All the way home.

Little Miss Muffet sat on a tuffet,
Eating some curds and whey;
Along came a spider, and sat down beside her,
And frightened Miss Muffet away.

Sing, sing! What shall I sing?
The cat's run away with the pudding bag string!

Little Polly Flinders
Sat among the cinders,
Warming her pretty little toes;
Her mother came and caught her,
And whipped her little daughter
For spoiling her nice new clothes.

Ding, dong, bell,
Pussy's in the well!
Who put her in?
Little Tommy Lin.
Who pulled her out?
Little Tommy Stout.
What a naughty boy was that
To drown poor pussy cat,
Who ne'er did any harm,
But killed the mice in Father's barn.

Trip upon trenchers, and dance upon dishes,
My mother sent me for some bawn, some bawn;
She bid me tread lightly, and come again quickly,
For fear the young men should do me some harm.
Yet didn't you see, yet didn't you see,
What naughty tricks they put upon me?
They broke my pitcher, and spilt the water,
And huffed my mother, and chid her daughter,
And kissed my sister instead of me.

Tom, Tom, the piper's son,
Stole a pig and away did run;
The pig was eat, and Tom was beat,
And Tom went roaring down the street.

Lucy Locket lost her pocket,
Kitty Fisher found it;
But ne'er a penny was there in it,
Except the binding round it.

Cushy cow bonny
Let down thy milk,
And I will give thee a gown of silk;
A gown of silk and a silver tee,
If thou wilt let down thy milk to me.

Goosey, goosey, gander, whither dost thou wander?
Up stairs and down stairs, and in my lady's chamber.
There I met an old man, who would not say his prayers;
I took him by the left leg, and threw him down stairs.

Cross Patch,
Draw the latch,
Sit by the fire and spin;
Take a cup,
And drink it up,
And call your neighbors in.

Pussy cat, pussy cat, where have you been?
I've been to London to look at the queen!
Pussy cat, pussy cat, what did you there?
I caught a little mouse under her chair.

January brings the snow,
Makes our feet and fingers glow.
February brings the rain,
Thaws the frozen lake again.
March brings breezes loud and shrill,
Stirs the dancing daffodil.

April brings the primrose sweet,
Scatters daisies at our feet.
May brings flocks of pretty lambs,
Skipping by their fleecy dams.
June brings tulips, lilies, roses,
Fills the children's hands with posies.

Hot July brings cooling showers,
Apricots and gillyflowers.
August brings the sheaves of corn,
Then the harvest home is borne.
Warm September brings the fruit,
Sportsmen then begin to shoot.

Fresh October brings the pheasant
Then to gather nuts is pleasant.
Dull November brings the blast,
Then the leaves are whirling fast.
Chill December brings the sleet,
Blazing fire and Christmas treat.

Ride a cock horse
To Banbury Cross
To see a fair lady upon a white horse;
With rings on her fingers,
And bells on her toes,
She shall have music wherever she goes.

Hickory, dickery, dock;
The mouse ran up the clock;
The clock struck One,
The mouse ran down,
Hickory, dickery, dock.

The hart he loves the high wood,
The hare she loves the hill;
The knight he loves his bright sword,
The Lady—loves her will.

One misty, moisty morning,
When cloudy was the weather,
I chanced to meet an old man clothed all in leather.
He began to compliment, and I began to grin,
How do you do, and how do you do?
And how do you do again?

One, two, buckle my shoe;
Three, four, shut the door;
Five, six, pick up sticks;
Seven, eight, lay them straight;
Nine, ten, a good fat hen;
Eleven, twelve, who will delve?
Thirteen, fourteen, maids a-courting;
Fifteen, sixteen, maids a-kissing;
Seventeen, eighteen, maids a-waiting;
Nineteen, twenty, my stomach's empty.

I won't be my father's Jack,
I won't be my mother's Jill,
I will be the fiddler's wife,
And have music when I will.
T'other little tune,
T'other little tune,
Prythee, love, play me
T'other little tune.

Heigh, diddle, diddle,
The cat and the fiddle,
The cow jumped over the moon;

The little dog laughed
To see such sport,
And the dish ran away with the spoon.

Intery, mintery, cutery corn,
Apple seed and apple thorn;
Wine, brier, limber lock,
Three geese in a flock,
One flew east, one flew west,
And one flew over the goose's nest.